AF606772

JAWS
OF THE NEW YORK BEACHES

Published by Arcadia Children's Books
A Division of Arcadia Publishing, Inc.
Charleston, SC
www.arcadiapublishing.com

Manufactured in the United States

Designed by Jessica Nevins
Images used courtesy of Shutterstock.com.

ISBN: 9781467197922
Library of Congress Control Number 2025930163

by Patricia Heyer

Adapted from
Shark Attacks of New York
by Patricia & Robert Heyer

Connecticut
New York
Long Island Sound
New Jersey
Long Island
Atlantic Ocean
5
4
3
6
4
6
1
1
4
5
1 & 5

Table of Contents & Map Key

WARNING
RECENT
SHARK SIGHTINGS
SWIM AT YOUR
OWN RISK

INTRODUCTION

What picture popped into your head when you first saw the cover of this book? Was it a beady-eyed, bullet-shaped beast aimed to attack? Did you snatch up this book to look inside, or did your hand hesitate for just a second before you pulled it slowly toward your face? Did you peek inside, fearful of what you might see?

If so, you are not alone. Most people admit that

they are afraid of sharks. Yet simultaneously, we can't get enough of these infamous apex predators of the world's oceans. Why else would we stand in long lines to watch blockbuster shark movies or binge-watch TV shows and videos? Why do we buy millions of dollars of shark-themed books, posters, clothing, and toys? We're so fascinated that we even dress up like sharks! Every Halloween parade has at least one ragged-toothed "shark" stalking the other trick-or-treaters as they stroll down the street.

Where does our fascination with sharks come from? Maybe we are intrigued with sharks because we are both top hunters—humans rule on land while sharks rule the seas. Or maybe it's that sharks have been swimming in our oceans for over 400 million years (that makes sharks even older than the dinosaurs!). With more than five hundred shark species found in the world's oceans, there are always new and interesting things to learn about them. In fact, the more we learn about sharks, the more interesting (and less scary) they become. Some sharks are as big as school buses, while others are smaller than your hand and glow in the dark. Some sharks never stop swimming, even when they sleep, and Greenland sharks can live to be five hundred years old!

But while some people find sharks fascinating, others find them downright *terrifying.* Many people fear sharks because movies and TV shows make them seem like scary bad guys hunting for humans—but that's not true. Sharks aren't mindless monsters; they are apex predators, and the ocean is their home. When we are in the ocean, anywhere in the world, sharks are closer to us than we realize. Sharks know you are there, and they usually don't care.

The truth is, of the millions of people who enter the water along New York's beaches every year, very few will ever have a run-in with a shark. (Fun fact: You are more likely to find a bug in your school lunch than you are to be bitten by a shark!)

That doesn't mean sharks aren't scary—they can be. (And warning: some of the stories in this book are scary, too!) But sharks are not the vicious monsters that movies and TV shows would have you believe. Rather, sharks are fascinating and curious creatures that help keep the world's oceans healthy.

So don't scream in terror and toss this book back on the shelf. Most sharks are not dangerous to humans and do not see people as prey. When a rare attack does happen, it's almost always because a shark has confused a splashing swimmer or surfer with an animal it usually eats, like a fish or seal. Sharks may take a nip to identify an arm or leg hanging from a surfboard or moving through

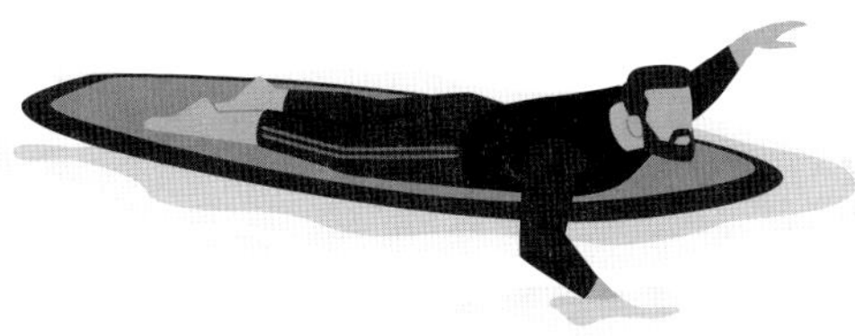

a wave, but they do not see us as a food source. (Unfortunately for us, even a nip from a shark can have serious consequences.)

In *Jaws of the New York Beaches*, you can read the accounts of what can happen when humans and sharks meet face-to-face. The results are not always what you might expect.

Some accounts have happy endings, and others sadly do not. As you read, you'll learn more about the sharks that inhabit our shoreline and better understand why sharks behave the way they do.

Some chapters are rather mysterious, and others will make you laugh, but they all share what can happen when a human and a shark come face-to-face. They will also remind you that it is *never* smart to swim alone or to annoy, tease, or injure a wild animal, especially a shark.

After reading these chapters, you'll learn why sharks need our protection now more than ever, and decide for yourself whether they really deserve their bad reputation. Be sure to check out the final chapter, where you can find lifeguard-approved

safety tips. These tips can help you "Swim Smart," preventing your day on the beach from being ruined by a shark encounter.

Whether you're splashing in the waves off Fire Island or surfing at Rockaway Beach, remember: when you enter the ocean, you are visiting a shark's home. Although New York's waters are usually safe, we are guests in shark territory . . . and must always enter at our own risk.

So, grab your bathing suit and read on! You will be surprised by who and *what* you will meet!

LET'S GO SWIMMING WITH SHARKS!

Do you like to swim in the ocean? If you do, you can honestly claim that you swim with sharks all the time! It's true. Anytime you head into the water to swim, surf, or just cool off, you are sharing the water with dozens of marine creatures, including sharks.

But just because sharks are often present in the water doesn't mean that swimming along the New York beaches is dangerous. It's true that encounters can happen (yes, even a nip from a shark's razor-sharp teeth can ruin your day), but most sharks are harmless and want nothing to do with people.

In the summer, a million people splash and swim at New York's beaches each and every day. Yet, did you know that in the last two hundred years, fewer than forty-five human–shark encounters have occurred in New York waters? That may sound like a lot, but don't panic! When you factor in the number of years and the number of people who have gone in the water, it's an *incredibly* low statistic. While the ocean is the sharks' home, swimming along our shores is safe.

But, as visitors to the ocean waters, we need to follow a few safety rules. Above all, we must remember to only swim when lifeguards are on duty.

In 1898, two Staten Island students learned that swimming on a beach without a lifeguard is never smart. It was so hot by noon one day that Charlie and Will couldn't stand being indoors another minute. When class was dismissed, they yanked on their shorts and raced to Prince's Bay.

Dropping their towels on the sand, they sprinted across the narrow beach and leaped into the cooling surf. They were floating just beyond the breakers when Charlie felt something whack his left leg. He laughed at first, thinking it was the piece of driftwood he had seen floating nearby. But he was wrong! His leg didn't hurt, so he didn't realize he was in trouble until he saw that the water around him had turned red.

Before he could speak, Will grabbed Charlie and tugged him toward the shore. By the time they reached the beach, Charlie's leg was throbbing. A huge flap of skin torn from his thigh was dangling over his knee, and a bloody goo was spewing down his leg, spreading across his foot and dripping onto the sand.

There was no one around to help, and Charlie couldn't walk, so Will hoisted him onto his shoulders and carried his friend all the way home. Although his wounds were serious, Charlie made a full recovery.

Since shark attacks are rare along the shores of New York, people don't always take them seriously—until they see the bloody results. That is what happened in Rockaway, Queens, on June 25, 1950. With schools closed for the summer, the beach was jam-packed. Beach umbrellas dotted the sand, and blankets were spread out everywhere along the beach at 103rd Street. Clusters of young children scampered across the sand, shouting and laughing at one another.

There were also older students in Rockaway that day, including a group from Newton High

School. The teens left their towels on the sand and quickly swam as far from the noisy youngsters as they could. They were laughing and splashing one another about 150 yards from shore when sixteen-year-old Joe suddenly bellowed," Help! A shark got me!"

The crowded beach was so noisy that only his buddies swimming nearby heard Joe's cry. Most thought he was being a wise guy and laughed. By the time they reached him, he was encircled in murky red water. They snatched Joe by his arms and towed him to the beach.

A crowd gathered as rescuers treated the wounded teen. At first, everyone was silent, staring as blood gushed from the ragged gashes on Joe's leg. Then someone stuttered, "Sh, sh, *shark*! "

People began to scream and shout,

running in every direction. Within minutes, the police arrived and whisked the injured teen away from the chaos to a nearby hospital. It took more than two dozen stitches to close Joe's wounds. It had been a close call—he was lucky to be alive.

Nearly seventy years passed before another shark attack along New York's beaches made headlines. July 18, 2018, was a day that Fire Island will always remember. Not only did two teens come face-to-face with a shark, but both attacks took place within minutes of one another and on nearby beaches.

Just before noon, thirteen-year-old Matthew was knocked off his surfboard on Atlantique Beach and bitten by a shark. (See the details in chapter two.) Then, just a few minutes later, a twelve-year-old girl crossed paths with a shark only four miles away on Sailors Haven Beach.

Lola, a seventh grader, was keeping cool in waist-deep water only ten feet from shore. Her father was standing in the surf watching her when he suddenly saw a panicked look come over her face. She wobbled a bit, losing her balance for just a moment before stumbling toward him with outstretched arms.

Lola's father dashed through the surf, meeting her just feet from the water's edge. He could tell by the bloody abrasions on her leg that she was badly injured. He scooped his daughter up in his arms and raced to the lifeguard stand. After a quick inspection of Lola's wounds, she was rushed to the hospital.

Her leg was a mass of cuts, gashes, and lacerations that spread from her knees to her foot. The wounds were so deep that the doctors did not stitch them shut. They were left open to be treated further to ensure proper healing.

The next day, Lola spoke with reporters during a press conference at the hospital. She calmly described how all she'd felt was a tug on her leg.

She declared that her leg hadn't hurt as long as it was submerged in the water.

Lola spoke bravely about her ordeal and showed that she had a good sense of humor. When a reporter asked," Did you realize a shark had bitten you?" Lola smiled and joked that she knew it couldn't have been a tiger. After all, she'd been at the beach when it happened. It had to have been a shark.

Following the two incidents, beaches along Fire Island were closed for the remainder of the day. Lifeguards were kept on duty until dark as patrol boats and drones scanned the shore for signs of sharks. Thankfully, no more sightings were reported that day.

While two shark run-ins on a single day are unsettling, anyone headed to the beach must remember that although sharks are common in our waters, attacks are rare. These apex predators are more afraid of humans than we know and usually try to avoid us if possible. Nevertheless, encounters can happen. In summer 2022, New York's beaches were back in the headlines.

The first week of July 2022 was busy as people prepared for the Fourth of July. Beaches were filled with happy vacationers looking forward to a long holiday weekend.

Just after lunch, a swimmer on Jones Beach rushed to the lifeguard stand with a jagged wound on his lower leg. He had not seen what had gnawed on his foot, but to the experienced lifeguards, it looked like a shark bite. As blood seeped from the edges of his wound, the swimmer was able to limp to the ambulance that took him to a hospital for treatment.

A few days later, on Friday, July 15, another run-in between a shark and a swimmer made news. Fire Island was gearing up for a busy weekend. At Seaview Beach, a tourist from

Arizona was in waist-deep water when a six-foot shark bumped against him and nipped his wrist before disappearing into deeper water.

The beaches were closed for several hours while drones scanned the surf for signs of sharks. By the time the beaches reopened, the Arizona man's wound had been treated, and he resumed his vacation. There were no more shark sightings along New York shores that summer, so no one was prepared for what happened the following summer.

The Fourth of July is the year's biggest celebration on local beaches. People began arriving by the first of July, filling the beaches all along New York with happy crowds anxious to celebrate our nation's birthday. Everyone expected large crowds, hot weather, and maybe a bit of sunburn. No one predicted that sharks would crash America's 247th birthday party. But they did!

The boardwalks all along the shore were

overflowing. Beach blankets and umbrellas were spread across the beaches so that you could hardly catch a glimpse of sand. Nearly every beach called in extra lifeguards, and drones took to the air to inspect the shoreline for signs of sharks. Despite all these safety efforts, six people along our shoreline would face a shark that week!

The first encounter took place on July 3 at Robert Moses State Park. A teenage girl was swimming with her friends when a sharp pain shot through her leg. She didn't know what was wrong, but she knew she was in trouble. Although her leg was throbbing, she swam to shore as fast as she could. By the time she reached the beach, blood was dripping down her leg onto her foot. She was taken to a hospital where her wounds were treated.

The next day was the Fourth of July. Just before eight o'clock that morning, fifty sand tiger sharks were spotted off Fire Island. Beaches all along the island remained closed for nearly two hours until the sharks had moved to deeper water. Yet before the day was over, first-aid teams would be rushing to treat four different shark attack victims.

The Fire Island shoreline was teeming with people that morning, and Cherry Grove was no exception. Some sprawled out on beach blankets, soaking up the sun, while others kept cool in the salty shallow waters. No one saw the four-foot shark until it was too late. One man was swimming close to shore when pain exploded

in his thigh. He paused for a moment to catch his breath, then swam as fast as he could for the safety of the beach. Blood oozed from his jagged wound, dripping down his leg and onto the sand.

The victim was rushed to a hospital for treatment.

A short time later, another Fire Island swimmer came face-to-face with a shark. This time, when the shark sank its teeth into the swimmer's thigh, she turned and battled the beast head-on. She beat on its snout, hammering and poking its eyes until it finally let go. Upon reaching the shore, the brave woman was rushed to a hospital where her wounds were treated.

The final two shark attacks of that Fourth of July took place on nearby Long Island beaches within six minutes of each other. At 1:50 p.m., a man was standing in the water near Quogue Village when a shark scraped against him, leaving a gash on his right knee. Then, just six minutes later, at 1:56, another swimmer at a nearby beach felt a vice-like grip on his wrist. He looked down just in time to see the shark disappear into the depths.

The shark attacks on the Fourth of July made

the front pages of local newspapers. Lifeguards used powerful binoculars to monitor swimmers, drones and helicopters scanned the surf, and patrol boats kept watch. No more sharks were sighted.

The final attack of the summer came three days later. A middle-aged woman swimming at the 59th Street Beach in Rockaway would be the victim of the most gruesome shark attack of the entire summer. She was several yards from shore when a piercing pain in her leg took her breath away. She glanced down to see that a shark had sunk its teeth deep into her thigh and was not about to let go.

The swimmer pounded on its snout and then used her bare hands to pry open its massive jaws! The moment she was free, she raced toward shore with a trail of bloody water following close behind.

By the time she staggered onto the beach, her lower body was drenched in blood. The first-aid team quickly applied tourniquets to slow the bleeding so she could be rushed to the nearest hospital. Newspapers reported that she was in critical condition, having lost twenty pounds of flesh from her upper leg. She did recover but would return to the operating room four more times before her massive wounds would heal.

Although most of the injuries from human-shark encounters are not serious, any shark bite can have life-changing consequences. No matter where we swim, it is important to *always* swim smart. Check out the last chapter in this book, "Swim Smart." You'll find a few lifeguard-approved safety tips to help keep you safe.

Wherever and whenever you swim, always swim smart!

LIFEGUARDS, SURFERS, AND THE SHARKS THEY MEET!

People come to the beach for many reasons. Some play games like volleyball or tag, while others stretch out on the sandy beach, soaking up the sun. Some splash about at the water's edge, while others can't wait to swim in deeper water beyond the breakers. Of all the people at the beach, one group stands out from the rest. They're not there to have a good time. They're there to do important work. They're the lifeguards.

If you look, you will see young men and women working as lifeguards all along our beaches. Often seated up high in their lookout towers, it may seem like they are relaxing in the sun and enjoying the cool ocean breeze, but nothing could be further from the truth. Being a lifeguard is hard work and a huge responsibility.

Lifeguards must always be alert, ready to race into the water the moment a swimmer appears to be drowning or in distress. Lifeguards must be expert swimmers and in good athletic condition. Every guard must be skilled in water rescue and first aid. To top it off, lifeguards must also be able to spot dangers lurking in the water, such as sharks!

In July 2022, two lifeguards encountered sharks during offshore ocean rescue training.

The first was the day before the big Fourth of July celebration on Smith Point Beach, Long Island, seventy miles east of Manhattan. That morning, Zac was helping other guards practice an important skill: rescuing a swimmer caught up in a dangerous riptide. A riptide is a powerful ocean current that can quickly pull swimmers away from the shore into deeper water.

Zac was pretending to struggle in the water when something suddenly smashed against his chest so hard that it took his breath away. He was an experienced lifeguard and knew at once what had happened.

When the five-foot shark spun around to attack, Zac was ready. He confronted the beast face-to-face, hammering on its snout with both fists. As the other guards raced to help, the shark turned and swam away. Despite puncture wounds to his chest and hand, Zac returned to duty the next day. When interviewed by the local paper, Zac reminded swimmers to never swim anywhere unless lifeguards are present.

Just one week later, on July 7, a shark confronted another Fire Island lifeguard. John was pretending to be a swimmer in distress when, suddenly, vice-like jaws clamped down on his left foot. He shrieked in pain and began to kick the shark's snout with his other foot.

By the time his teammates reached him, the shark had vanished. John's injuries were not serious, although it took more than six stitches to close the gash on his foot, and he could not report for duty for more than a week.

Surfers are another group you will likely spot on local beaches. Just as it takes lifeguards skill and practice to save a drowning person, riding a surfboard as it glides atop a wave isn't as easy as it looks. Although almost anyone can learn to surf, it takes a lot of practice—and it is important to learn to surf correctly.

Surfers, like lifeguards, often use a buddy system whenever they are in the water. They know not to surf where people are fishing or when schools of baitfish are near the shore, since apex predators may be following close behind.

Surfers and lifeguards may use secret nicknames to tell one another that a shark has been spotted. If you hear a surfer say that he saw "the man in the gray suit," you know a shark has been sighted, and it's time to get out of the water.

Hundreds of surfers can be seen along New York shores every year, from Rockaway to Montauk. Although most come during summer, you may see surfers even on the coldest winter day. On a frigid January day in 2007, two men clad in black wetsuits carried their surfboards toward Smith Point Beach. Both were experienced surfers and always used the buddy system, especially in frigid waters. Before paddling their boards beyond the breakers, they scanned the surface for any signs of danger.

Wayne was resting on his nine-foot board when something bumped him. He looked around but didn't see anything unusual. Then, out of the corner of his eye, he saw that a shark had taken aim and was headed straight for him.

He began shouting and pounding on the water to make as much noise as possible. Just when the two oversized black eyes were inches from his face, the creature veered away, disappearing into deeper water. Wayne and his surfing buddy left the water immediately.

Surfers didn't report any more shark sightings

or attacks for another eleven years. But in July 2018, a thirteen-year-old boy named Matthew was riding his boogie board near Atlantique Beach on Fire Island when something slammed into him, knocking him into the water. As Matthew popped back to the surface, his leg exploded in pain. It was like nothing he had ever felt before. "It wasn't sharp; it was just kind of a shock," Matthew later told reporters. "Because it was really quick. It was one second, and then it just let go immediately." He wasn't sure what was wrong, so he headed straight for the safety of the beach. As Matthew stumbled onto the sand, lifeguards saw the blood gushing down his leg.

EMTs arrived and quickly removed a shark tooth from Matthew's wound before rushing him to the hospital. During an interview the next day, Matthew insisted the shark bite had felt more like an electric shock.

It was almost four years before another surfer

and shark crossed paths in New York waters. In July 2022, an eighteen-year-old surfer named Max was resting on his board in shallow water near Fire Island when suddenly, his leg felt like a giant wrench was squeezing it. Just then, his attacker let go, and Max jerked his leg to the surface. He took one look at the bloody four-inch laceration and made a mad dash for the beach. Although no one saw what had bitten him, everyone agreed it was a shark bite.

Fourth of July 2023 will be remembered for many years as the day that sharks were unwanted guests at our national birthday party. (Chapter 1 shares the stories of the five swimmers who were victims of shark attacks on that holiday.)

Did you know there was another victim that day? A surfer named Peter encountered a predator while catching a wave on Fire Island's Kismet Beach. It's not certain if Peter knew about the shark attacks earlier that day, but around six o'clock, he was resting on his board when something in the water suddenly latched on to his foot. He shouted and kicked at his attacker until it let go and swam away.

Another surfer saw Peter struggling in the water and rushed to help. By the time they reached the safety of the beach, blood was dripping from the lacerations on Peter's foot and toes. Peter recovered quickly and, before long, was once again "hanging ten" on Fire Island.

For the next ten days, drones scoured the shore for sharks, helicopters flew overhead, and extra lifeguards scanned the beach for signs of trouble. There were no more shark sightings until July 13, when a sand tiger shark came to visit.

Shawn, an experienced surfer, knew the beaches of Fire Island like the back of his hand. Although he knew the safety rules of surfing, he'd taken a chance when he headed out into the surf at 7:30 that evening on an unguarded beach. He was fourteen yards offshore when, suddenly, something knocked him off his board. When Shawn opened his eyes, he saw the menacing face of a giant sand tiger shark.

Just as the shark moved into position to charge, Shawn hopped back onto his board. A wave passed by seconds later, and Shawn rode it back to the safety of shallow water. Although his left calf was bleeding, his wounds soon healed.

Whether you love to have fun in the ocean or are there for a job, safety should always be a top priority. The ocean is a powerful place, and it must be respected along with the many creatures that call it home—especially sharks. When we enter their territory, we need to remember it is their home, not ours. Always practice ocean safety, stay aware of your surroundings, and enter at your own risk.

And while most people only look for sharks in the ocean, here's something surprising: sharks can swim in other places, too! Would you believe that some of New York's most historic (and harrowing) shark stories happened right in our local rivers? Read on to learn more, but be warned: you may never look at the Hudson and East Rivers the same way again!

NO SWIMMING

BEWARE THE RIVER SHARKS!

What pops into your mind when you hear there has been a shark attack? A jagged tooth beast chomping down on a helpless swimmer on a crowded New York beach? Or maybe a fisherman who falls from a boat into the path of a hungry ocean shark? But did you know that some of the most extraordinary shark attacks in New

York didn't take place in the ocean at all? They happened in New York City in the Hudson River and East River waters.

These waterways are some of the busiest in the world, with dozens of vessels from around the globe entering New York's rivers daily. Swimming is not popular in our rivers today due to pollution and heavy commercial traffic, but this has not always been true.

New York had grown into a busy city by 1860, with businesses, workshops, and factories lining the riverfronts and more than a million people calling New York home. Although both the Hudson and East Rivers were soon polluted, swimming and fishing were widespread. Those living along their banks continued using the rivers as the only way to cool off on a hot day.

The summer of 1860 was not a happy one for most people in America. The entire country had been on edge since April when the Civil War had broken out. When summer arrived a few months later, a heat wave sent the temperatures soaring into the high nineties. For most New Yorkers, there was no escape from the relentless heat.

Many families living near 11th Street in Brooklyn worked as day laborers from dawn to dusk. With low wages, most people lived in tenements (small, tightly packed apartments without indoor toilets, running water, or electricity). When temperatures soared, it was impossible to keep cool. The residents' only escape from the oppressive heat was to wade or swim in the nearby rivers.

One sweltering August day, a man named Mr. Duke left his job early at the Brooklyn Navy Yard at six o'clock. He hurried home to share supper with his family. When the meal was over and the dishes were being cleared, Mr. Duke leaned over to his nine-year-old son Jerry and whispered, "How about we take a dip in the river and cool off a bit?" A grin spread across Jerry's face; he sprang from his chair and ran to grab his shorts.

They hurried down the few blocks to the swimming spot on the East River. When they arrived, they were greeted by neighbors already splashing about along the edge of the murky-colored river. Jerry and his dad were good swimmers, so they dove right into the water and swam away from the others. They were floating on their backs when suddenly an earsplitting shriek echoed across the water. Jerry bellowed, "Daddy! Daddy! Something bit me!" His Dad turned to reach for him, but all he could see was his son enclosed in a circle of reddish-brown.

Mr. Duke wrapped his arm around Jerry and swam as fast as he could to the nearest shore. By the time they reached land, Jerry was sobbing so hard that he could hardly breathe. His father eased him onto the sand and quickly wound his shirt around Jerry's foot to stop the bleeding. But it was no use. Blood was spewing from what was left of Jerry's big toe. He yanked Jerry onto his shoulders and raced the entire way home.

When Jerry's mother saw his wound, she washed and wrapped his foot before giving him a large tablespoon of a nasty-tasting brown liquid. Word of the attack spread across Brooklyn like wildfire, and soon, an old woman arrived carrying a worn burlap bag bulging with dried plants, wedges of bark, and odd-shaped twigs. Everyone knew the elderly lady as Grandma Nonna. Grandma Nonna delivered nearly all the babies in the neighborhood and was on-call whenever someone was sick or injured. She treated people with her homemade medicines made of herbs, leaves, and twigs. In those days, doctors were expensive, and there was no such thing as an emergency room.

Although Jerry screamed in pain, Grandma

Nonna cleaned the wound once more with a greenish-yellow liquid. Then she spread smelly wilted leaves across Jerry's toes and wrapped them tightly in a clean cloth. When she was finished, she told Jerry's mother to make a big pot of strong tea and give it to Jerry whenever he cried.

His mother nursed him as best she could, but Jerry was in terrible pain. Back then, there were no medicines to prevent infection and few painkillers to ease his throbbing wound. Jerry spent the next two months in the hot, stuffy apartment, waiting for his toe to heal.

When a reporter from the *New York Times* came to their home, Jerry's father refused to let them interview Jerry. Although the reporter didn't meet Jerry, he left the injured boy a large bag of caramels from a fancy Manhattan candy shop. It took a long time, but Jerry recovered. He never swam in the East River again, but thanks to the friendly reporter, he learned to love caramels.

It was only four years later, in 1864, with the Civil War raging all around, when another shark attack took place in a New York river. This time, it happened on Manhattan's west side, in the Hudson River.

New York Harbor was bustling with more ships than ever because of the war. The docks were jammed with raw materials coming in by the ton, and millions of military supplies shipped out each day. Shark sightings were surprisingly common despite being such a busy harbor, especially around 38th Street. (Today, it is the site of the Javits Center.)

Large animal slaughter docks, known as offals, lined the riverbanks. Cattle, sheep, horses, and pig carcasses were butchered and prepared for sale. The entrails, skins, and blood were dumped into the river. This is what likely attracted sharks to the area.

Sharks were the last thing on thirteen-year-old

Henry Brice's mind that hot August evening as he headed to the harbor to catch a cool breeze and watch the ships loading and unloading cargo. He was standing on the dock when two sailors rowed up in a small rowboat. He was thrilled when they asked Henry if he would watch their boat while they got supplies for their ship. The sailors told Henry he could row around a bit and even take a swim if he liked, as long as he was careful not to lose their boat.

At first, Henry rowed away from the dock for a few minutes. But it was so hot that he soon decided to take a quick dip to cool off. He grabbed the long rope tied to the bow of the rowboat and then tied the other end around his waist using a strong double knot. He checked the knot again before easing into the water.

Within seconds, his ankle seemed to explode as massive jaws clamped down on his leg. Henry took one raspy breath before his shrieks of pain echoed across the water. Flinging his body toward the boat, he tried to swim. He didn't get more than a few feet before the shark latched onto his left leg. Just as he grabbed hold of the rowboat, the shark leaped from the water and once again sunk its bloodstained teeth into his thigh. The pain took his breath away, and the water around him turned red.

Somehow, Henry managed to pull himself back into the boat. He lay at the bottom, watching the blood spewing from his body. His ankle was a bloody mass of ragged muscle and tissue, and his left leg was ripped open the length of his thigh. Worst of all, a massive chunk of flesh was missing from his right thigh to his knee. No matter where he looked, all Henry saw was blood. Then, he passed out.

Two fishermen saw the attack and rushed to help. They tore off their shirts and made tourniquets to try to stop the bleeding. Just then, the shark returned and rammed their boat, biting off a piece of the railing. The fishermen yanked Henry into their boat and raced for the shore.

The men carried Henry to his home, where a doctor fought throughout the night to save his life. News of the attack spread quickly throughout Manhattan. Soon, a crowd gathered outside his window, waiting for word about the boy's injuries. So many people gathered that the police came to keep people from blocking the streets.

In the morning, Henry was still alive, but he was critically injured. In 1864, there were no antibiotics to kill infection and few pain medicines to ease suffering. A few days later, Henry had to endure another surgery to remove two pounds of rotting tissue from his thigh before he began to heal.

He couldn't leave his apartment for more than

six months, and it took two years for him to be able to do everyday things like run or play ball. Although some newspapers offered him money for an interview, Henry and his family refused to discuss the attack. Henry recovered and grew up to become a skilled mason who helped build the Elevated Railway in Manhattan, but he never again swam in the Hudson River.

The same summer as Henry Brice's attack, when the Civil War was raging across America, a boy named Charlie Gates was born in nearby Brooklyn. Fourteen years later, in 1878, Charlie became the next victim of a river shark attack in New York. This time, the attack was fatal.

Charlie and his fifteen-year-old pal, Artie, lived in Brooklyn near the river. When their friends said that the best place to catch crabs was upstream, the two friends scraped up enough money to rent a rowboat and try their luck in deeper water just offshore.

They carried their crab traps, a bucket, and a net down to the boat landing near their home. While Charlie counted out the coins to pay the boat fee, Artie loaded their equipment into the rowboat.

The friends rowed upstream away from the shore, where they had heard the best crabs were caught. After they dropped their traps into the

water and let them sink to the bottom, they settled down to wait.

Charlie and Artie had expected it to be cooler on the water, but they were wrong. The sun beat down on their bare heads, and soon, they were dripping in sweat. That is when Charlie decided to take a dip to cool off. Artie refused. His father had warned him that the river was too dangerous for swimming.

Charlie shrugged his shoulders, peeled off his clothes, and rolled over the side of the rowboat into the water. He let himself sink just a bit before he opened his eyes. There, staring at him eye-to-eye, was a shark. A very big shark!

Charlie shot to the surface, but he was not fast enough. Just as his head broke above the water, the beast clamped down on his hip with its huge razor-sharp teeth. Charlie bellowed in pain.

Artie couldn't believe his eyes. A huge grayish shark was shaking Charlie as if he were a rag doll. Artie yanked on the oars and raced to help his friend. When he was close enough, Artie grabbed the rock they were using as an anchor and smashed it into the eye of the frenzied beast.

The shark eased its grip on Charlie just long enough for Artie to grab his wounded friend and yank him into the rowboat. Charlie lay in a heap at the bottom of the boat. Blood spurted from his wounds, forming pools of red in the bottom of the boat.

The moment Charlie was safe onboard, Artie headed for shore. He had never rowed so hard or fast in his life. His arms burned, and sweat poured down his face. It felt like he had rowed for miles before he reached the nearby fishing dock.

An ambulance was called, but the police thought it was a hoax, and instead of an ambulance, they sent a policeman to check out the call. It was forty-five minutes before an ambulance finally arrived to rush Charlie to the hospital.

His wounds were severe. More than a pound of flesh had been ripped off Charlie's midsection and hip. For nearly a week, he drifted in and out of consciousness, sometimes thrashing about as if reliving his fight with the shark. On August 13, Charlie died from his wounds. The eight-foot perpetrator, believed to be a bull shark, was never caught.

Today, nearly one hundred and fifty years since that fateful summer, swimming in the Hudson River and East River is still considered unsafe in most places. Hundreds of large cargo ships move about on the rivers daily, the pollution level remains high, and although they are seldom spotted, sharks can enter the rivers any time they choose. Officially, it is not against the law to swim in these rivers . . . but would you really want to take that chance?

HELP! THERE'S A SHARK ON MY LINE

Do you like to fish? If so, the New York shore is the perfect place to go. You can catch fish with your feet firmly planted on the ground, or cast your line from the deck of one of the dozens of fishing boats docked at marinas all along the shore. Private fishing vessels, charter boats, and a huge local commercial fleet are all searching for fish. You can reel in a fluke, flounder, cod, striped bass, or tuna.

But while saltwater fishing can be thrilling and fun, there is a lurking danger to consider. At any moment, you could find yourself in a face-off with the ocean's apex predator, the shark! Although most sharks pose little to no threat to humans, a close encounter with one can quickly turn your fishing expedition into a heart-pounding adventure.

Captain Jack Kelly, an experienced Montauk boat captain, shared his story of an ill-fated fishing trip from 1941.

The sun was shining brightly that hot August day when Captain Jack and his pal, Quince, guided their small fishing boat out of Montauk Harbor and headed for the fishing banks off-shore. They hoped to snag a couple of flounders or, if they were lucky, a nice-sized striped bass. They dropped anchor and cast their lines into the water as soon as they arrived.

Suddenly, Jack's line tore from his reel as a powerful force latched on to his bait. As he battled to reel in his catch, the giant creature continued to rip the line from his spool and bolted away. Jack jerked his pole upward to set the hook. This was no ordinary fish. It was a real fighter!

For two long hours, Jack fought to bring the mighty fish to the surface. Again and again, he released *just* enough line so that the creature thought it had escaped. Then, Jack would reel in the line as fast as he could, bringing the fish closer and closer to the boat.

The battle was taking a toll. Jack's face was drenched in sweat, pain shot down his back, and his arms burned as though they were on fire. Finally, he spotted the huge gray mass coming to the surface. With painful cramps shooting through his hands, Jack grit his teeth. He cranked the wooden handle on his reel even harder, bringing the six-foot shark right alongside the boat. The fight had taken its toll on the shark, too. The beast stared blanky ahead, motionless in the water with its giant jaws agape.

Although this was not the striped bass he had hoped for, Captain Jack knew it was a trophy catch. He was so anxious to show off his prize to his pals onshore that he quickly roped the dead shark to the side of the boat and hurried back to port.

When Jack and Quince reached the dock, they slipped a noose around the shark's huge tail and hoisted it into the air. It hung there for more than four hours as news of the catch spread along the waterfront. Before long, a newspaper reporter arrived. Jack was delighted when asked to pose for a photo with the giant shark.

Captain Jack stood close to its toothy snout

and flashed his proudest grin. But then—just as he reached to point out the animal's gaping, distorted mouth—the shark lurched sideways! It sunk its teeth into Jack's arm, slicing it open in one long bloody gash. Blood spurted across Jack's face and clothing. The shark was *not* dead, and no one was more surprised than Captain Jack.

Jack was rushed to the local hospital, where it took over a dozen stitches to close his wounds. Later, when the *New York Times* asked him what he had learned from his experience, Jack replied, "Never trust a shark!"

Another fisherman who came face-to-face with a shark wasn't in a boat; he was in the water spearfishing in Oyster Bay, off Long Island's North Shore. Bruno had been in the water for half an hour and had already caught five good-sized blackfish when he spied the shark.

Without thinking, he quickly fired his speargun. The three-foot-long spear pierced the shark's thick skin. It passed completely through the shark's body before emerging on the other side. The stricken creature thrashed and convulsed, unable to escape the fishing line that connected it to Bruno's speargun. When its attempts to swim away failed, the shark spun about to defend itself against the spearfisherman.

Bruno realized too late that spearing the shark had been unwise. The wounded beast heaved itself against its attacker in a battle for its life. Bruno tried to grab the shark by its gills, but it was too late. The shark buried its teeth into Bruno's leg, clutching him in a vice-like grip.

Although Bruno screamed in pain, the shark did not relent. It jerked and thrashed, ripping away the fisherman's flesh in giant gulps. When Bruno tried to make the shark let go by beating on its snout, the shark latched on to Bruno's hands, gnawing them into a bloody mass.

Bruno's friends saw what was happening and

raced into the water to help. They quickly killed the shark and rushed Bruno to a nearby hospital, where four shark teeth had to be dug out of his leg before his wounds could be closed. Bruno's right hand didn't look like a hand at all. His bloody fingers and flesh were mangled beyond recognition. His left hand was bleeding heavily, and all that was left of his thumb was a small stub. Although Bruno had many surgeries to heal his wounds, his hands never healed completely.

The ocean is a shark's natural habitat and home. When we enter ocean waters, we need to remember that we are only visitors. Though most sharks avoid humans, they—like *any* wild animal—will fiercely defend themselves if they feel threatened. Attacks on humans are rare, but when they do happen, we must know how to quickly retreat!

A man from Queens narrowly escaped a shark attack one hot August day in 1884 by making a clever yet speedy retreat from the shallow waters of Jamaica Bay. Stephen was hunting for hard clams in four feet of water off Mill Basin Beach. Using a long-handled clam rake, he swept the sea bottom, pulling the rake closer and closer each time. When the rake reached his feet, he jerked it upward and plucked several hard clams from its prongs.

Then, suddenly, Stephen got an eerie feeling. He looked up just in time to see a six-foot shark rocketing straight at him. At the last moment, the shark swerved, sideswiping Stephen and nearly knocking him off his feet. The shark vanished, only to reappear moments later.

This time, Stephen was ready. As the shark

sped toward him a second time, Stephen held the rake out to block himself from the oncoming attack. When the shark was within reach, Stephen struck the beast on its snout as hard as he could. Once again, the shark darted away.

His heart pounding, Stephen stood facing the open water with his back to the shore. He held the clam rake with both hands, waiting for another attack. Never taking his eyes off the water, he began inching his way backward to the safety of the beach.

The gray streak bulleted toward him for the third time, only to be met by the iron prongs of the rake. Stephen moved slowly backward, inch by inch, until the water barely reached his ankles.

It was then that the shark seemed to realize its predicament. The water was so shallow that it couldn't swim away. Its belly scraped along the sandy bottom, and its large, triangular dorsal fin stuck out of the water. The shark thrashed and heaved about for a few minutes. Then, it flipped its great body backward through the air, landing in deeper water farther from the shore. In an instant, with a frenzied, final splash, it disappeared. Stephen's quick thinking and calm response helped him escape a possible shark attack.

Though the risk is low, we know that shark encounters can happen anytime we enter their territory. Just like we're careful when hiking in the woods or mountains, it's smart to respect the ocean and remember that we are guests in this amazing underwater world. Sharks do not see people as prey, but they are wild animals and apex predators. Accidents can happen. The danger increases if humans provoke sharks by teasing, hassling, or injuring them. This was the case when a scuba diver, John, poked a shark with his harpoon on a fateful Saturday in 1958.

It is an unusual story because scuba diving was not a well-known sport at that time. The famous French ocean explorer, Jacques Cousteau, had invented the complicated equipment needed for humans to breathe underwater just a few years earlier. Only the military and a few highly trained divers knew how to use SCUBA (Self-Contained Underwater Breathing Apparatus) gear safely.

Even in modern times, the use of SCUBA equipment is complicated, requiring extensive training and practice. Divers must carry their own supply of oxygen in tanks strapped to their backs, and they rely on highly specialized equipment to ensure it functions properly.

We do not know how long John had been a scuba diver or how well he was trained. We only know he was diving off Staten Island, New York City's southernmost borough, when he spotted a shark. He fired his speargun, striking the shark just above its pectoral fin. (Pectoral fins extend from behind a shark's gills and are used for steering.)

The shark went into a wild frenzy when the spear made contact. The beast thrashed and flailed, swimming wildly in circles while entangling John in a giant knot of heavy fishing line. Each time the shark circled, the knot around John's body got tighter and tighter. Before John realized what was happening, he was trapped underwater and could not move.

Just as he reached for his knife to slice away the web of knots, the shark bolted for the open ocean at full speed, dragging John behind. All he could do was hold on to his mask and air mouthpiece to keep them from being ripped off his face.

The shark dragged John more than a mile from shore before he could fight his way to the surface.

John knew he had to do something or he would surely drown. He let go of his mask long enough to grab his knife and began to slice through the web of knotted lines trapping him.

The moment the line was cut, the shark disappeared into deeper water, and John slipped out of the air tank harness. He floated on the surface until he spied a nearby boat and was able to signal for help.

Some accounts claim that the shark bit him during the frenzy, although no details of his injuries are known. We do know that John got the ride of a lifetime. One he will never forget.

MISSING WITHOUT A TRACE

Have you ever seen a magician make a rabbit vanish before your eyes? Or watched a chilling scene from a suspenseful movie where someone suddenly disappears without a trace? The stories you are about to read don't have anything to do with movies or magic. They are real-life mysteries about *real* people who have gone missing along the New York coastline, leaving no clues or explanations behind.

When this happens, people often assume that a shark must have eaten the victim. But shark attacks on humans are rare and almost always a case of mistaken identity. Sharks do sometimes attack and bite humans, but we really aren't on their menu. They prefer smaller fish, seals, and other kinds of marine life. But remember, even a nip from a shark's razor-sharp teeth can ruin your day at the beach.

Although it doesn't happen very often, people *have* vanished without a trace in New York's waters. One of the first stories reported was 382 years ago, when New York was still known as New Amsterdam. This was when the Dutch had settled the area and were trying to defend their colony from English invaders.

War broke out between the Netherlands and England when the English tried to take over New

Amsterdam. In 1642, the English naval fleet was spotted near the harbor. The governor of New Amsterdam sent out messengers to the soldiers stationed around the area to prepare for battle.

One of these soldiers, Anthony Van Corlaer volunteered to warn the troops stationed ten miles away in the Bronx. Anthony knew there was no time to waste. He leaped on his horse and headed north. It was a long, hard ride on horseback, and the approaching thunderstorm didn't help.

All Anthony could hear was the pounding of his horse's hooves as they thundered across the hard dirt roadway leading to the Spuyten Duyvil Creek crossing. He stopped and stared across the water when he reached the creek bank. Anthony's heart sank. It was high tide; the water was too deep for him to cross. He looked everywhere for a raft or rowboat, but there was nothing he could use to carry him across the creek.

Anthony knew his mission was vital. He had

to get across to warn the soldiers on the other side. People cheered as he took a deep breath, leaped into the creek, and began swimming for the far shore. But tragically, he would never make it that far. When he was halfway across, people on the creek bank began to scream and call to him. Anthony had vanished right before their eyes. No one saw him struggle or heard him call for help. He was gone without a trace.

Two hundred years later, in August 1858, Prince's Bay, Staten Island, was the site of not one but *two* cases of sudden disappearance. Not only would they occur within three days of one another, but they would also take place on the same beach!

On Saturday, August 28, three twelve-year-old

boys finished their chores and raced to the beach. They were seen heaping their clothes into a big pile on the sand and then chasing one another into the surf. They were last seen swimming about forty yards from shore.

When the boys failed to come home for supper, their families began the search. Friends and neighbors joined in, and they hunted throughout the night. But there were no sightings of the three swimmers, and their bodies were never recovered.

Some fishermen reported seeing sharks in the bay earlier that week, but there was no evidence to explain what might have happened. The three friends had vanished without a trace.

The mystery deepened three days later on

August 31, when another Staten Island man disappeared while swimming on the same beach. Like the three boys just days before, he walked down to the beach, dropped his clothes on the sand, and swam away, never to be seen again. Witnesses saw him swimming forty to fifty yards from shore. Then, suddenly, he was gone. There had been no cry for help or disturbance in the water. He had simply vanished.

The most famous account of a mysterious disappearance along our shores took place in June 1964. Britt Sullivan, a well-known long-distance swimmer, was determined to make the record books. Twenty-nine years old, Britt's goal was to swim three thousand miles across the Atlantic Ocean from New York to England. She believed it would take her five months to complete the trip if she swam for eighteen hours every day.

Britt entered the water on Coney Island on

June 26, wearing a black wet suit with yellow stripes and dark fins. She had a flashlight, a dye marker for emergencies (carried so rescue teams can easily spot a person in the water), a canteen, and a knife. She swam from shore and headed along the southern coast of Long Island, heading north for Montauk. Along the way, her escort boat kept watch from a quarter to half a mile away.

On the first night, Britt left the water for the safety of the boat when her team spotted a shiver of sharks prowling in her pathway. Once the sharks left the area and the danger had passed, Britt resumed her swim.

There were no more shark sightings that night. By night two, Britt had reached the eastern edge of Fire Island and was heading to Montauk Point. At a rest spot near the Fire Island buoy, she signaled her escort boat to move ahead a quarter of a mile to their next meeting site. Little did she know, Britt would never make it to the site, and she would never be seen alive again.

When Britt failed to arrive, her team began searching along the path she had been following. They traced the route again and again, but there was no sign of Britt. They radioed to other vessels in the busy waters, but no one had seen her. Soon, the Coast Guard took up the search, scouring the water with helicopters and boats. There was no trace of the long-distance swimmer.

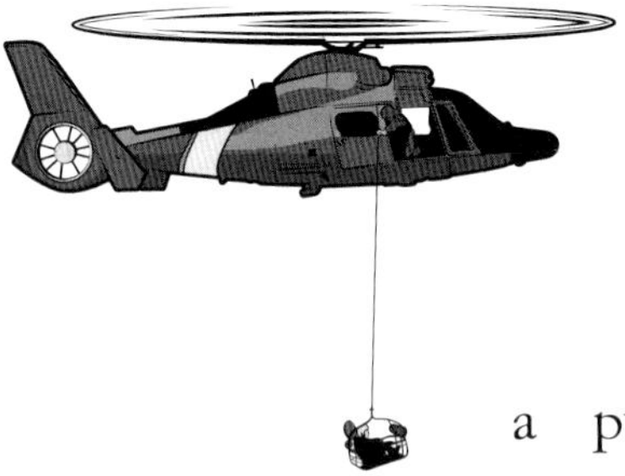

Some people said it was a publicity stunt, which is something done just to get the public's attention. They expected Britt to reappear shortly afterward, but she was never seen again. To this day, nobody knows exactly what happened to her. Perhaps she drowned. Or maybe she came face-to-face with an unfriendly shark. The truth is, we will most likely never know. All we know for certain is that on June 27, 1974, Britt Sullivan disappeared without a trace—a good example of why no one should *ever* swim alone. After all, even expert swimmers can go missing.

STRANGE & CURIOUS SHARK ENCOUNTERS ALONG OUR SHORES

There have been forty-five reported shark attacks along New York's shores since 1642. A few reports differ from the others. These stories are so strange that you may not believe them—or they might even make you laugh!

You'll read about three sailors who claimed to have been chased by *thousands* of angry sharks.

You'll meet a courageous Civil War veteran who only survived a shark attack by being transformed into a mummy! In a final story, you'll need to decide if the killer culprit from the famous 1916 Matawan shark attacks may have escaped to Sheepshead Bay, only to confront a new group of local swimmers. (Or . . . was the whole thing just a spooky, *sharky* coincidence?) You'll have to read on to find out!

CHASED BY A MOB OF SHARKS!

You might not be that surprised to be chased by the class bully, a stray dog, or even a hive of angry bees. But would you expect to be chased by an angry mob of sharks?

Although a group of sharks is properly called a shiver, you may see other words such as school, herd, or even frenzy used to describe a group of sharks. In this case, the three sailors insisted that a mob of sharks chased them!

The weather on Sunday, July 2, 1880, was perfect for sailing along New York's southern shore. Alex invited his two pals, George and John, for an afternoon sail across the Narrows to show off his newly outfitted sixteen-foot skiff.

The Narrows, known as the Gateway to New York Harbor, is a narrow stretch of water between Staten Island and Brooklyn. It is the busy main channel for all shipping into New York City. It is deep water with constant wind and strong tides.

That Sunday was perfect for a leisurely sail; the Narrows was less crowded than on a weekday and the blustery breeze could not have been more perfect. The little skiff skimmed across the water in the bright sunshine. The three young men stretched out across the deck, enjoying the warm breeze.

In the middle of their conversation, Alex pointed out an odd-shaped dark spot on the water's surface, just off their port side. It didn't look like anything they had ever seen. Anxious to get a better look, they rearranged the sails, changing their course toward the hazy dark form.

As the men grew closer, they saw the mysterious spot was bigger than they'd thought. It was an enormous black mass that kept changing shape.

A sudden burst of wind pushed the skiff ever closer to the unfamiliar mass. By the time they identified the mysterious blob, it was too late. They had sailed into a giant shiver of sharks!

Within seconds, the skiff was surrounded. Hundreds of ragged-tooth snouts protruded from the water, inching closer to their boat. Some beasts circled the craft in endless loops while others scraped their jagged teeth against the side of the wooden skiff, inches from the terrified sailors. The men grabbed the seat cushions and began smacking the sharks' menacing snouts. But that did not scare them away.

Then, suddenly, a huge shark emerged from the gray mass and rammed the skiff. The small boat shuddered as it lurched sideways, allowing seawater to drench the three men. It was all they could do to keep the skiff afloat.

Before they could speak, a shark leaped from the water and landed across the width of their boat, nearly hitting Alex in the face! The sound of splintered wood echoed across the water as the boat plunged beneath the surface under the weight of the giant beast. At that moment, the shark jerked away and disappeared.

The damaged skiff looked like it was about to sink, when suddenly, it popped upright, revealing the three men clinging to the handholds along the side of the boat. They managed to climb back onboard and thought they were safe. But then they saw water seeping into the hull through a large gash. They were in big trouble; they had to get to land quickly, or they would be lunch for the hungry sharks.

Alex adjusted the sails and headed for the nearest shore. George tried to plug the hole with his jacket, and John bailed water with a small lunch box. As they raced for safety, dozens of sharks trailed them, swimming inches from the stern. It wasn't until they reached Bay Cliff that the sharks finally gave up the chase. The skiff limped into the harbor, with three sailors happy to have survived.

Although the men insisted there were thousands of sharks in the "mob" that chased them, most reports that day say the shiver of sharks was likely several hundred, not several thousand.

What do you think? Do you think it would be difficult to keep count if you were in a small boat amid a mob of angry sharks? And really, does it even matter if it's hundreds of sharks versus thousands of sharks chasing you? Either way, that's *way* too many sharks!

THE MUMMY WHO SURVIVED A SHARK ATTACK

This is the account of a mummy who survived a shark attack. It isn't the kind of mummy you might see on a visit to a museum, nor is it the kind of mummy you might create using toilet paper or fabric strips for a Halloween party. This mummy was very much *alive*. In fact, being made into a mummy is what saved his life! Curious? Read on.

It happened on Long Island in early September 1865. Although the Civil War had officially ended that spring, many troops were still trying to find their way home. Peter Johnson was nineteen and had been in the war for three years. He enlisted when he was sixteen and fought in several battles until he was wounded at Spotsylvania. When doctors released Peter from the hospital that summer, he began to make his way back to his home in Maine.

Peter found his way to New York, where he got a job as a deckhand on the sailing schooner, *Catherine Wilcox*. He was thrilled with his good luck because the boat was bound for Eastport, Maine, just forty miles from his home.

The schooner left Southold with the tide and sailed north along the coast. As they reached the Eastern edge of Long Island, the winds suddenly died. The great sails of the ship lay limp, and the schooner bobbed helplessly in the water, its journey halted until the winds returned.

For a little while, there wasn't much for the crewmen to do but wait for the wind to pick up again. The crew roared with laughter when Peter suggested they take a swim now that their chores were finished. No one was willing to join him, and some even teased him, calling him "fish bait" as he stepped over the rail and dove head-first into the water.

The moment his head was underwater, Peter opened his eyes. To his confusion—and then terror—he saw two huge black discs staring back at him. Peter was face-to-face with a giant shark. The shark clamped down on Peter's waist swiftly and plunged to the bottom. Peter was holding his breath and trying to fend off his attacker when the shark suddenly released its grip. In a panic, Peter swam desperately to the surface, gasping for air.

But the fight was not over. The shark was right behind Peter and latched on to him once more. The crew of the *Catherine Wilcox* looked on in horror as the shark flung Peter around like a rag doll in a spray of frothy red water.

Despite his grave predicament, Peter was

not about to be lunch for a shark. In an act of desperation, he shoved his thumb deep into the shark's eye socket. The shark let go, and Peter bolted for the ship. Once again, however, the jagged-toothed beast followed. The shark sank its teeth into Peter's body. This time, tragically, the shark bit off a large chunk of Peter's abdomen.

After much effort, the crew heaved Peter's mangled body onto the deck. Without a breeze, the *Catherine Wilcox* was helpless; there was no way to get Peter to shore. The crew wrapped him in a blanket and laid him on the bottom of a rowboat, then rowed eight miles to the nearest land in Greenpoint.

The doctors had little hope that Peter would survive. His wounds were severe, and he had lost a great deal of blood. They decided it was hopeless and planned to make him as comfortable as possible until he passed away.

Somehow, even in his dire state, Peter was still conscious. He realized what they were doing and asked Dr. Skinner to try to save him. When the doctor told him it would be too painful, Peter replied, "Please, just give it a try." Although Dr. Skinner thought it was useless, he promised to do his best.

Peter's body was so badly injured that it didn't look much like a body at all. It was a shapeless mass of bloody tissue, hanging skin, and broken bones. But nevertheless, having promised Peter he would try to save him, the doctor sent for a giant ball of wire. The only thing he could think to do was wrap Peter's body tightly with the wire and see if it held together.

By the time the doctor finished, Peter looked like a mummy encased in wire with small openings left for him to eat and see. Despite the dreadful pain, Peter had barely made a sound.

He was put to bed and checked on every fifteen minutes just to see if he was still alive.

The next morning, Peter greeted Dr. Skinner by asking, "When can I go home?" The doctor could hardly believe what he was seeing. Somehow, Peter had miraculously survived the night. But his situation was still critical. Wounds covered his entire body. He could not sit up for three weeks and remained in the hospital for nearly three months. He had to learn to walk again, and his body was seriously damaged from the attack.

Just before Christmas, Peter left the hospital unassisted and returned to Maine in time to spend the holidays with his family. Although he carried horrific scars and injuries from his battle with the shark, it did not keep him from living a full, productive life in his hometown of Robinson, Maine.

More than ten years later, newspapers still carried the story of Peter's encounter with the fifteen-foot great white shark and how he survived by becoming a *living* human mummy.

A SCARY CONNECTION TO A SUMMER OF SHARK TERROR!

Whenever people talk about shark attacks, no matter where they are, they always end up talking about the famous shark attacks of 1916 in nearby New Jersey.

It is sometimes called the summer of terror because in the span of just twelve days, four different shark attacks occurred in four different shore towns. More than five people were injured, and four people lost their lives. It all started on June 30, when a shark bit a teenage swimmer in Atlantic City. The very next day, on July 1, just a few miles north, a young man in Beach Haven lost his life in yet another shark attack. Five days later, on July 6, just a few miles north of Beach

Haven, a hotel worker in Spring Lake was killed by a shark as he swam on a hotel beach.

The worst was yet to come. On July 12, a shark attack in Matawan, New Jersey, made the national news. In a single day, three people were seriously injured, and two more were killed in the most famous shark attack in American history.

When dawn broke the following morning on July 13, they were still searching for the body of the boy killed in the Matawan attack. Little did anybody know, just fourteen miles away in Sheepshead Bay, two New Yorkers would also come face-to-face with a shark.

In the days before TV or radio, only those who had read the morning paper would have heard about the Matawan shark attacks. It is unlikely that the two New Yorkers about to meet a shark were aware of the danger in the waters.

It was mid-morning at the waterfront Beau

Rivage Hotel on Emmons Avenue in Brooklyn when Thomas, a steward at the hotel, decided to take a dip in the bay before the luncheon rush. Thomas was an avid swimmer, but during the busy tourist season, he had to sneak in a swim whenever he could. Just as he reached the beach, he spied his pal, Joe, and shouted to him to join in a quick dip in the bay.

When they reached the shoreline, they discovered one of the hotel's boats was available. They clamored aboard and rowed beyond the breakers to swim in cooler, deeper water.

Thomas peeled off his shirt and dove in. Just as Joe was stripping off his shirt to join him, he spotted the telltale dorsal fin closing in on Thomas. "Shark!" he screamed. His shriek echoed all along the beachfront, causing swimmers to rush out of the water.

Thomas lunged for the boat and was about to

pull his legs over the side when he felt a sandpaper scrape on his ankle. He hurled himself over the edge and landed in the bottom of the boat with a thud. When he looked down, he saw a bloody scrape seeping blood on his foot.

Joe manned the oars and rowed them back to shore as quickly as he could. Thomas's wound was not serious. He received first aid. Shortly after the lunch rush, he returned to work.

Just minutes later, another swimmer came face-to-face with a shark in nearby Sheepshead Bay. Gert was a dancer who exercised daily swimming in the bay near her home. She was about a hundred yards from shore when she spotted a large dorsal fin protruding from the water.

Gert remembered reading a newspaper article about how to scare away sharks while swimming. She faced the shark head-on and began thrashing about, splashing water in every direction, making noise, and beating on the surface with her hands. Suddenly, the fin changed direction and swam away.

Gert didn't waste any time; she swam to shore and reported her encounter to the authorities. She was not injured, thanks to the tips she learned from the newspaper article and her quick thinking and courage.

These two shark run-ins are peculiar, perhaps even spooky, because they happened in New York waters, less than fifteen miles from the murderous attacks that had just taken place in nearby Matawan. The killer shark was never captured, so we will never know if that same predator was the one hunting in New York waters the very next morning. What do you think?

SHARKS: A BIG FISH WITH A BAD REPUTATION

Sharks have a bad reputation. It doesn't matter if you watch a blockbuster movie, a television show, or are scrolling YouTube; sharks are almost always cast as the bad guys. Have you ever noticed that the music gets louder and louder as you watch the shark circling the unsuspecting swimmer? Then a gory close-up shows razor-sharp teeth, a jagged fin slicing through the water, and a look of terror in the swimmer's eyes . . . just before the water turns red.

Every summer, during Shark Week on the Discovery Channel, the TV is filled with dozens of shows about sharks. A few teach us about the lives of sharks, but most are filled with gruesome footage of fictional shark attacks. Even real-life shark videos are often edited to make the shark encounter seem more threatening, but this is not an accurate portrayal. In reality, humans kill far more sharks (roughly 100 million per year), than sharks kill people (fewer than ten deaths per year). It seems like maybe *sharks* are the ones who should be making scary movies about us, and not the other way around!

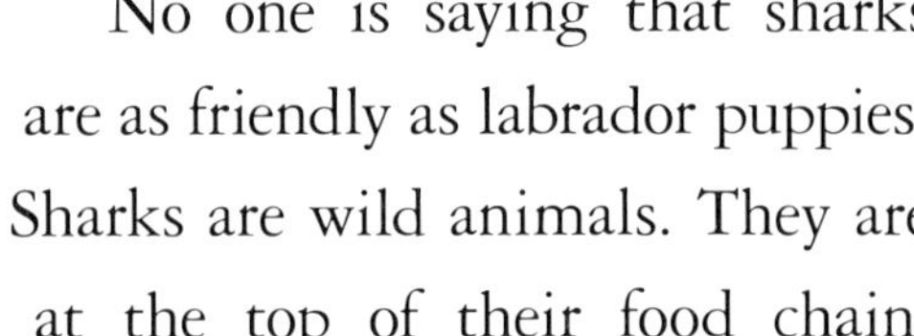

No one is saying that sharks are as friendly as labrador puppies. Sharks are wild animals. They are at the top of their food chain, hunting and eating anything they

choose in the world's oceans. But sharks are not the villains of the sea. They are just doing what sharks have done for more than 400 million years. And though they have a bad reputation, scientists know sharks are not only essential to the health of the world's oceans—but the world itself.

As apex sea predators, they help keep the food chain balanced so all sorts of creatures can exist in the world's oceans. If sharks disappeared, it would start a chain reaction in the ocean. Without sharks, seal populations would multiply too quickly. Too many seals would eat too many small fish, leaving bigger fish hungry. Before long, many ocean species would vanish, and the ocean's ecosystem would fall out of balance, badly affecting all life on Earth—including humans.

As you've read in this book, shark attacks *do* sometimes occur, even along the beaches of New York. When that happens, it can be a tragic, life-changing event. Though there are more than five hundred different kinds of sharks, only a few are known to attack people. Even a curious nibble can indeed be dangerous or even fatal for a human, but sharks do not see people as prey, nor do they hunt humans as a food source. Just as you would rather skip the mystery meat at school, a shark would much rather feed on fish and other marine animals than you. Small sharks eat shrimp, krill, crabs, and small fish. Larger ones dine on bigger fish, seals, turtles, whales, and even seagulls.

Perhaps we are not on the shark's menu because we taste like the cheeseburgers and French fries we eat. (That is good news.) In most cases, when a shark bites someone, it is a case of mistaken identity. They see arms and legs thrashing about in the water, and they simply mistake it for prey. But try not to worry. After all, more people die every year from skydiving accidents, runaway lawnmowers, dog bites, lightning strikes, rip currents, and even falling coconuts than from run-ins with sharks. (So, you know, look out for falling coconuts!)

And instead of seeing sharks as the bad guys, try to see them for what they really are: critical members of our planet's ecosystem. Without them, the health of the world's oceans would quickly deteriorate.

It's fun to watch scary shark movies or TV shows. But remember, many of them are just entertainment and are not usually accurate. Stop by a library or go online and learn about the different kinds of sharks and their behavior. You will see that these unique sea creatures are both fascinating and essential members of the world's food chain. You will be surprised by what you find out!

Here are some fascinating facts to get you started:

Did you know that a shark is a fish, and like other fish, sharks have skeletons—but *unlike* other fish, the shark's skeleton is not made of hard bone? A shark's skeleton is made of cartilage. Cartilage is a bendable material that is strong but not hard like bone. (Like your ears, or the tip of your nose, for example.)

Sharks also come in many sizes and personalities. They can be twenty feet long like the Greenland shark or as small as six inches like the dwarf lanternshark. Some sharks are shy and seldom come near land, while others love to roam near the coastline. Some are fearful of humans and rush away; others are more curious and sometimes aggressive.

Some sharks migrate, traveling long distances each year, and some never stray far from where they were born. Some sharks stay where the water is warm, and others love the cold water of the Arctic. Some sharks lay eggs, and others bear babies alive.

Some sharks, like the Greenland shark, lumber

along at a mile per hour, while others, like the shortfin mako, zip through the water at nearly thirty miles per hour—with bursts of speed up to forty-six miles per hour!

Although sharks are not known to be able to make sounds, they do have all the other senses. They can see, hear, smell, and touch. In addition, they have a unique sense known as *electroreception.* It enables the shark to know when living prey is near. (A very handy tool for a predator.)

A shark's jaw stores rows and rows of razor-sharp teeth just waiting to move into place whenever a tooth is lost. During its life, a shark may grow as many as thirty thousand teeth! (No wonder some people call a shark's mouth "the business end of a shark!")

Some sharks are endangered, including the great hammerhead shark, sand tiger shark, sandbar shark, and blacktip reef shark, among others. Due to the media's negative portrayal of sharks, overfishing, and cruel practices like shark finning, shark populations have declined. But there is still plenty of hope, and educating yourself about sharks is one of the best ways to help them.

Sharks do not live up to their bad reputation. Swimming and surfing along New York's shores is safe. But we need to remember that the ocean is full of marine creatures of all kinds, and it is their home. We are only visitors. When we enter their world, we must be smart and courteous guests.

Although seeing a shark in the wild as it swims through the waves is a sight you will never forget, it could ruin your beach day should you actually cross paths. Check out the final chapter, "Before You Go," where you'll find some lifeguard-approved tips for swimming safely on our beaches.

BEFORE YOU GO: ALWAYS SWIM SMART!

Everyone needs to "Swim Smart!": It doesn't matter if you are a beginner, intermediate, or expert swimmer.

While most sharks along New York shores are harmless, we must remember that shark attacks can happen. When they do, it can swiftly become a life-and-death situation. Here are some lifeguard-approved safety tips for all beachgoers.

1. Never swim alone.

2. Never swim anywhere without lifeguards.

3. Always follow lifeguards' instructions. They aren't playing around when they tell you to get out of the water. That means there is danger.

4. If you see a fin sticking out of the water, get on shore and tell a lifeguard.

5. Avoid swimming at dawn or dusk, when sharks like to feed.

6. Don't swim where there are schools (large groups) of baitfish. Larger fish, such as sharks, are often chasing these fish.

7. Return to shore immediately if you see a large or unusual animal in the water. It is better to be safe than sorry.

8. Don't wear shiny jewelry or play with shiny objects in the surf—it may attract sharks.

9. Never tease or injure an animal of any kind.

10. If you see a sick or injured fish or shark, do not touch it. Report this to an adult.

Remember: ALWAYS SWIM SMART!

Patricia Heyer is a local history buff with a special interest in New Jersey folklore and marine science. She has written extensively for both children and adults. Her most recent title, *The Ghostly Tales of Nantucket,* was released in 2024. Pat is an avid reader, beachcomber, and animal rescue supporter. She resides on the Jersey Shore with her husband, Rob, and their rescue cat, Gracie. Visit www.heyerwriter.com to learn more!

Dive into even more books by Patricia Heyer!